READY FOR REVIVAL

A 40-Day Heart Journey
Toward the Fullness of Christ

JACQUIE TYRE

A *Pray!* Magazine Book

Pray! Books • P.O. Box 35004 • Colorado Springs, Colorado 80935
www.praymag.com

Pray! magazine books are published by NavPress. NavPress is the publishing ministry of the Navigators, an international Christian organization whose mission is to reach, disciple, and equip people to know Christ and to make Him known through successive generations.

Printed in the United States of America

4 5 6 7 8 9 10/ 06 05 04

Dedication

In the journey of pursuing God for revival, God has blessed me with marvelous friends who have a similar passion for His manifest presence. Some of these are long-time prayer partners, family friends, fellow members of our local congregation, or instantaneous heart-friends from prayer gatherings or conferences. Each holds a very special place in my heart, for through them God has greatly enriched my life.

Still others have come along, and God has granted us the special privilege of becoming partners in ministry, co-laborers in the journey. The Servant Leadership Team of UniteAtlanta qualifies in a unique and special way. This group of friends and co-laborers began walking together in early 2000, daring to dream of a revived church that would make a significant impact on the millions of people in the beautiful metropolitan Atlanta region.

In the summer of 2000, after hosting our first major event with Ed Silvoso, our team met for a few days to discover and define our purpose statement as a ministry. What emerged from those days continues to stir us all to excitement and anticipation. The purpose statement of UniteAtlanta says that "we are a movement of pastors, intercessors, and worship leaders rallying the church to transform our city with the presence of Christ." By God's grace, we continue to pursue our God-given purpose in hopes of seeing transformation become more than just a word on our lips.

While each year we embark upon a variety of initiatives, none seemed quite as monumental as calling the church in the city to forty days of prayer, repentance, and fasting late in the summer of 2001. After setting our objective and the dates, the team looked my way and commissioned me to write a forty-day prayer guide that could be distributed throughout the city. With fear and trembling, I accepted the challenge and began to pray, "Lord, help!" Indeed, He did.

Initially, we anticipated that we could distribute one thousand copies; but God had far larger plans. Thanks to the generosity of some significant church supporters of UniteAtlanta and a local advertising agency, Larry Smith & Associates, 4,100 copies of this guide—then called *A Call to Prayer, Fasting and Repentance for the Church in Atlanta*—were distributed across the city. God moved among us, drawing us closer to Himself and to one another with a fresh love for our city.

It was with great joy that the leadership team of UniteAtlanta blessed this opportunity to have *Pray!* Books publish and distribute this prayer guide under its new title, *Ready for Revival*. The underlying desire of our team is that whatever God has given us, we want to freely share with others as a blessing and encouragement for advancing Christ's kingdom.

I would like to dedicate this book to the Servant Leadership Team of UniteAtlanta with love and gratitude for trusting me with this project a year ago, and for releasing it to me for this publication. Thank you, Team—Joel Balin, Walter Gilbert, Fred Hartley, Randy Haviland, David Wayne Lawrence, Marc Lawson, Cecil Ross, David Shiff, Chris Strong, Donn Thomas, and Carl Wilhelm. You guys are the best!

Thank you, also, to my wonderful husband, Mike, and sons, Aaron, Nathan, and Justin. This project could never have been completed without your patience, love, and encouragement. I love you very much, and pray that you will know God's reviving presence and the joy of serving Him always.

My prayer is that the Lord would use this guide richly to prepare us for the coming revival with greater revelations of His marvelous love, and His desire for us all to walk in holiness and the fear of the Lord. May He continue to transform us all more and more into the likeness of His dear Son, Jesus Christ—our Lord and Savior.

For His glory—now and always,

Jacquie Tyre
Atlanta, Georgia

Introduction

All across the land talk of a needed or perhaps imminently pending revival can be heard among believers of all denominational and non-denominational groups. Sometimes the conversations reflect an urgency of desperation, or a sense of expectancy that revival could break out any moment. In still others, the word revival conjures up fears of the unknown, or doubts that genuine revival is a possibility in our culture. Regardless of the perspective you will be hard-pressed to find someone who does not, at least to some degree, believe we need revival—and that perhaps the events of our day point to a revival sweeping our land in the near future.

Even the news media seems to be picking up on the awakening of spirituality, of a growing hunger and desire for God. Shortly after the tragedy of September 11, 2001, Peter Jennings said "Prayer is becoming the fabric of the church in North America." Major magazines and newspapers have, of necessity, carried articles on the growing role of prayer in our society. God is up to something—and people, believers and non-believers alike, are noticing.

An honest look at the church today convicts me that we are indeed desperate for a fresh move of God to return us to biblical Christianity. Scripture clearly teaches that unity among believers is to be pursued; strife, division, and contention are to be forsaken; and holiness is to characterize our every action and attitude. Still, the church in community after community continues to struggle with the consequences and evidences of sin. Pastors leave the pastorate at alarming rates; divorce rates in the church meet or exceed that of the unchurched; congregations split over personal preferences; substance abuse occurs more often than most want to admit; and our youth often leave the fold to look for spiritual reality outside the church of their parents.

Where is the hope? We are living in the largest historical prayer movement of all times—God's people are praying. A revival of prayer and worship continues to grow among youth and young adults at an amazing rate. Twenty-four-hour-a-day, seven-day-a-week worship and intercession centers are springing up all across the country. Congregations gather together for worship, prayer, and outreach events across denominational, ethnic, and worship-style lines. City-reaching movements such as Mission America, the Lighthouse Movement, and Prayer Summits continue to grow in significance all across the land.

The Holy Spirit is stirring the church to prepare herself. The church in various cities is beginning to respond with corporate calls for prayer, repentance, and fasting. God's people are responding in heartfelt desperation, crying out to be purified and prepared for an out-pouring of the Holy Spirit in revival power. God is answering—but we know there is more.

While each community or city has its particular issues of sin and strongholds of resistance to the gospel, *all* need an increased measure of the character of Christ. If revival is to come to our land, it must begin among God's people—His church. And it must begin with individuals who want to be revived spiritually—you.

This prayer guide offers a way, based on God's word, to lead individuals, congregations, or city-wide ministries through a process of heart-searching response to God's call to "Prepare the way of the LORD, Make His paths straight" (Mk. 1:3, NKJV).

Whether you are embarking on this journey alone or as a part of a city-wide initiative, step out with hope and expectancy, for God has promised that when His children "humble themselves, and pray and seek [His] face, and turn from their wicked ways, then [He] will hear from heaven, and will forgive their sin and heal their land" (2 Chron. 7:14, NKJV).

Are you ready for revival? Are you hungry for more of Christ's fullness in your life? Are you willing to ask the Lord to prepare your heart for revival? Do you desire to be positioned to receive and live in the reality of His reviving presence? Do you yearn to see your community transformed with the presence of Christ? If your answers are yes, then turn the page and see what God has in store for you and your community.

Almighty Father, move in us, among us, and through us to perfect Your work and purposes in Your church. We yield to You, O Lord, trusting that You will lead and guide us in the way we should go. Lord, we come to You seeking revival that will transform our cities to increasingly reflect Your glory and honor to all nations. We ask this not for our sakes, but for the sake of Your holy Son, Jesus Christ, and for the advancement of Your kingdom. Father, let Your kingdom come. Let Your will be done in the cities of the world as it is in heaven. In Jesus Christ's name we pray. Amen and Amen.

A Call to Fast and Pray

"'Now, therefore,' says the LORD, 'Turn to Me with all your heart, with fasting, with weeping, and with mourning.' So rend your heart, and not your garments; Return to the LORD your God, for He is gracious and merciful, slow to anger, and of great kindness; And He relents from doing harm. Who knows if He will turn and relent, and leave a blessing behind Him—A grain offering and a drink offering for the LORD your God?" (Joel 2:12-14, NKJV)

Throughout Scripture, spiritual leaders called God's people to times of fasting and prayer when the need for transformation was recognized. Fasting demonstrates the desperation and sincerity of our hearts in approaching the Lord our God. It is a tangible expression of humility, acknowledging our utter dependence upon the Lord.

Pray! Books and I highly recommend that you add some form of fasting to your forty-day experience. God will bless your act of faith.

Seek the Lord to instruct you as to how and what He wants you to fast for this season in your life (see Is. 58:6-14). Whatever fast you choose, be careful that it is faithfully added to extended seasons of prayer. We offer the following options as suggestions for your consideration:

1. Juice only
2. Fresh fruits and vegetables only (a Daniel fast)
3. Fast one day per week for the six weeks
4. Fast one meal per day
5. Fast a particular food or activity as a token of your devotion and commitment

Pray that this time will be radically used by the Lord to bring life transformation to us all—personally and corporately—throughout your church and city.

Editor's Note: You will notice that plural pronouns (us, we, our, etc.) are used throughout this prayer guide. We do this to give you a sense that you are not alone in your prayers for revival. Even if you are not a part of an official group that is praying this together, undoubtedly there are many believers in your community, and perhaps in your church, who are regularly praying for revival.

How to Use This Guide:

Reflect: Read the suggested Scriptures, asking the Holy Spirit to speak to you and reveal to your heart how He wants you to respond, personally and on behalf of the church in your city.

Repent: The written issues are merely suggestions others have gleaned from the Scriptures and from times in the presence of the Lord. *Respond only as the Lord gives you liberty and genuine conviction.* This is an opportunity for both personal repentance and intercession for the church (see Nehemiah 1 and Daniel 9). Make note of the issues of repentance the Lord leads you through.

Receive: First John 1:9 says: "If we confess our sins, he is faithful and just and will forgive us our sins and purify us from all unrighteousness." It is important to receive forgiveness and grace in order to turn to God's ways. Ask for and receive what the Lord releases to you by faith, for yourself and for the church, to live out a life of repentance that is turned from sin.

Revive: Pray and intercede for the specific work of revival that is revealed in the daily focus. This is an act of revival prayer, not just praying for revival. It is praying for God's revealed will and purposes for you and the church in the name of Jesus Christ our Lord. Daily inquire of the Lord as to what He would have you pray for His church.

Rejoice: Close with a time of thanking, celebrating, and praising God for who He is, what He is doing and what He will yet do in and through His church. Intentionally close your time of prayer looking toward Jesus Christ, the author and finisher of our faith.

SECTION 1

Our Relationship with the Lord Our God

The first area we must deal with is our personal and corporate relationship with the Lord. Throughout Scripture we see that our first and primary responsibility is to the Lord and that out of the condition of that relationship all others will flow. If we are to impact those around us with the love of Christ, we must first live in a growing love relationship with Him.

This week,
we will focus on our primary pursuit—that of loving
the Lord our God with all our heart, all our soul,
and all our strength, and allowing His love to transform us
more and more into the likeness of Jesus Christ.

Sat.

Day 1

Loving God

Reflect: Read Dt. 6:1-9; Mt. 22:34-40

Repent: Of not loving God with all our heart, soul, mind, and strength; of allowing other things to fill and occupy our lives; of not loving and teaching others the ways of the Lord; of

_____

_____

Receive: Forgiveness and receive His love in a fresh measure (1 Jn. 4:19).

Revive: Intercede for the church in our community to be filled with fresh love for God and to demonstrate His love to those around us—both in the church and among those who do not yet know Christ. Pray that the love of Christ would compel believers everywhere to share the gospel with others in love.

Rejoice: Celebrate the love of God, by faith proclaiming that His love will transform our lives more and more into the image of Christ and will touch our city with His redeeming presence.

Day 2

Seeking the Lord

Reflect: Dt. 4:39-40; 2 Chron. 7:12-16; Heb. 11:6

Repent: Of not consistently seeking after the Lord to know Him, His ways, His will, and His plans; of seeking after the ways and approval of man; of being complacent or lethargic in pursuit of the Lord; of being satisfied with the mediocrity that comes with the familiarity of religious form and tradition; of

_____

_____

Receive: Forgiveness and ask for a fresh impartation of holy, passionate diligence to know the Lord, to see His face and to walk in communion with Him. Receive a fresh glimpse of His beauty and fresh faith that comes from setting your heart to seek after the Lord.

Revive: Intercede for the church in our city to turn and seek the Lord with a whole heart; to allow the pressures of our day and of our society to draw us into a deeper place of earnestly pursuing the Lord; to walk in fresh desperation to turn from our wicked ways and return to the Lord with a whole heart, desiring to see His glory in our day—in our city and nation.

Rejoice: Praise the Lord for His promise to hear from heaven, forgive our sin, and heal our land. Praise Him for His faithfulness and mercies that are new every morning.

Day 3

Obeying His Commands

Reflect: Dt. 11:18-32; Jn. 14:15-24; 1 Jn. 4:20-5:3

Repent: Of professing to love God without obeying His Word (commands); of presuming upon God's love and mercy by persisting in known, revealed sin; of failing to love others when God's Word declares that we can't love God without loving our brother; of making excuses for not obeying His commands; of expecting God's blessings without obedience to His commands; of _____

_____

Receive: A passion for the Son of God that makes us long to obey; forgiveness and grace from the Lord to obey His Word; love and joy in keeping the Lord's commands, for they are not burdensome but full of life and blessing.

Revive: Intercede for the church in our city to be filled with a love for the Word of God; to receive the Word of God with joy; to hear the Word, not according to the letter of the law which is unto death, but according to the Spirit unto life; for the commands of the Lord to be preached in truth and love; for the church to demonstrate the blessings of the Lord's commands in our communities—that the world might see that His ways are good and full of love.

Rejoice: Join with King David, the psalmist, agreeing by faith with Ps. 40:8—that our delight is in the Lord and that we delight to do His will.

Day 4

Waiting on the Lord

Reflect: Psalm 62; Is. 40:31; 2 Thess. 1:2-10

Repent: Of anxiety and impatience; of activity born of the flesh to make something happen and not born of the Spirit unto faith; of looking to anything or anyone else for what only God can supply; of trusting in human strength, ingenuity, or creativity rather than waiting patiently on the Lord and His ways; of _____

_____

Receive: Forgiveness and a fresh impartation of the Holy Spirit to patiently wait on the Lord and His ways; eager anticipation from the Lord for His plans, purposes, and timing to be revealed in our days.

Revive: Pray for the church to receive eager anticipation that is full of faith and hope to wait for the Lord's will to be revealed; to be still and know that the Lord is God and that He will be exalted among the nations; He will be exalted in the earth (Ps. 46:10); to trust fully in the Lord, knowing that He knows the times and the seasons and is able to accomplish that which concerns us today; to walk in the freedom of waiting on the Lord—mounting up with wings like eagles, running and not growing weary, and walking without fainting.

Rejoice: Delight in the Lord that His faithfulness is our hope, and that the promises "are 'Yes' in Christ. And so through him the 'Amen' is spoken by us to the glory of God" (2 Cor. 1:20).

Day 5

Following after the Lord

Reflect: Psalm 63 (especially v. 8); Josh. 14:8-9; Lk. 9:23-26
Definitions to Consider—*Follow*
(Heb. *Strong's* #1692): to impinge, i.e., cling or adhere; fig. to catch by pursuit:—abide, fast, cleave (fast together), follow close (hard after), be joined (together), keep (fast) . . . pursue hard.
(Gr. *Strong's* #190): to be in the same way with, i.e., to accompany (spec. as a disciple):—follow, reach.

Repent: Of clinging or adhering to anything or anyone other than Christ; of pursuing worldly, fleshly affections; of following the ways of man and culture rather than the Lord; of protecting the self-life rather than going the way of the cross; of inconsistency in pursuing the Lord and His ways; of pursuing success and self-promotion rather than the Lord's way of self-denial and death; of __

Receive: Desperation of heart for the Lord to replace the complacency and distractions of this world; purification of heart motivation; restoration of first-love passion for Jesus; a fresh anointing to follow the Lord.

Revive: Pray for the church to become passionately committed to following after the Lord; to become wholly devoted to the Word of God and His purpose; to "throw off everything that hinders and the sin that so easily entangles, and let us run . . . the race marked out for us" (Heb. 12:1); to return to the message of Christ to take up our cross and follow Him—daily; to enter into a fasted life of denying self and the youthful passions of this age; to have the Holy Spirit pour out holy passion for Jesus upon the church that would fuel our pursuit of Him; to recognize that Jesus is worthy of all our affection, all our pursuit, and all our devotion.

Rejoice: In the Lord's provision of grace to follow Jesus, thanking Him that it is not up to us to provide what is needed—we must only respond to His Spirit's prompting us within. Hallelujah! "He who began a good work in you will carry it on to completion until the day of Christ Jesus" (Phil. 1:6).

Day 6

Inquiring of the Lord

Reflect: Judges 20 (especially references to inquiring of the Lord); Ps. 27:4-5

Repent: Of not inquiring of the Lord regarding what He desires, or the direction He would have us go; of not inquiring of the Lord regarding instructions and strategies for ministry; of presuming to know His ways and His will without asking of Him; of waiting to inquire of the Lord until a time of crisis; of

_____

_____

Receive: A fresh impartation of His Spirit of grace and supplication to inquire of the Lord (Zech. 12:10); a desire and devotion to know the will of the Lord; a purity of devotion to wait for His will and providence to be revealed in all things.

Revive: Pray for the church to recognize every way in which we go forward in our own strength without inquiring of the Lord; a fresh stirring of the Holy Spirit in the church to inquire of the Lord before stepping forward in intercession, outreach, or any type of ministry; a transformation of the ways of ministry that plan first, and then ask God to bless, rather than inquire of the Lord for direction, instruction, and empowerment.

Rejoice: That it is God who works in us both to will and to do for His good pleasure (Phil. 2:13); that He is faithful to answer us when we call upon Him and show us great and mighty things we do not know (Jer. 33:3); that He is always faithful.

Day 7

Serving the Lord

Reflect: Psalm 100; Zeph. 3:9; Heb. 9:11-15, 12:28-29

Repent: Of serving without joy or unity of the Spirit with brothers and sisters in the body of Christ; of serving out of law and not love; of serving with impure intentions, goals, or reasons; of serving for selfish gain, attention, or advancement; of serving without holy reverence or outside of obedience to Christ's commands to our heart; of serving _____

_____

_____

Receive: Grace and mercy from the Lord, releasing us from the bondage of sin confessed and releasing us into the purity of service born of simple devotion to Christ; a fresh anointing to serve with joy, gladness, unity, purpose, purity, passion, and power for Christ's name sake and for the advancement of His kingdom.

Revive: Pray that the church would be filled with gratitude, love, surrender, passion, and obedience to serve the Lord with gladness and with one accord. Pray for the church to be found faithful serving the Lord out of the purity of love, not simply out of a sense of obligation or good works; that our service would be God-motivated, God-centered, and God-ordained to reflect His life in our homes and community.

Rejoice: That He who calls us is faithful to enable and empower us to serve according to His will and His purposes; that He is worthy of our service and a loving Master who loves His servants, not a hard taskmaster.

SECTION 2
Our Relationships with Our Family

Our secondary arena of responsibility lies within our nuclear family. The family unit has suffered great assault over the past several decades. Sadly, Christian families suffer much of the same destruction as those who do not know Christ as their Savior. We must begin to deal honestly with the sins within our homes. God intended for our homes, particularly our marriages, to be demonstrations of His love to the world.

This week,
we will seek the Lord regarding our relationships within the home—husbands, wives, parents, and children. May God lead us into His more perfect way of love.

Day 8

Loving One Another in the Family

Reflect: 1 Corinthians 13; Eph. 5:25-33; Col. 3:19; Titus 2:4; 1 Jn. 4:11,20-21

Repent: Of not loving one another according to 1 Corinthians 13, especially within the family unit; of loving conditionally based on performance, behavior, or other expectations or criteria; of failing to demonstrate love to our family members, taking them for granted or presuming upon each other in ways that dishonor; of _____
_____

Receive: A fresh cleansing from the sin of not loving as Christ loves; an impartation of His love for you that will touch those closest to you in the family.

Revive: Pray that husbands would truly love their wives as Christ loves the church—protecting, supporting, and encouraging them to be all God created them to be in Christ Jesus; that wives would learn to love and honor their husbands in ways that will encourage, support, and build them up as the head of the home—privately and publicly, particularly before the children; that as parents we would love our children unconditionally—demonstrating this love with encouragement, time, and healthy boundaries of discipline; that children would love their parents with honor, respect, and obedience; that the love in homes would reveal Christ to the community.

Rejoice: That God, who loves us each completely and perfectly, will enable us to love one another by His grace; that Christ so loves us and our families that we can trust Him to build love into us.

Day 9

Submitting to One Another

Reflect: Eph. 5:15-24; 1 Pet. 3:1-2, 5:5; 1 Tim. 3:4; Jas. 4:7

Repent: Of failing to submit to one another in the fear of the Lord; of resisting God's ordained order for the family unit—as husbands, wives, and children; of misapplying the idea of submission by overbearing dominance over one another; of lack of submission to God demonstrated in lack of submission to one another, particularly to those in authority over us in the Lord; of _____

_____

Receive: Forgiveness and restoration of relations of holy submission to one another; fresh grace to live submitted to the Lord and to one another in our families.

Revive: Intercede for God's Spirit to bring forth a revival of pure submission within our families; for God's divine order to be established within family units throughout the church in our city; for God's blessing to be poured out upon families that live according to God's order of unity; for the world to see the blessing and benefit of families living in godly order and submission.

Rejoice: That God's way is the way of blessing for our families; that He is able to purify and perfect divine order within our families; that He is the Lord of our families.

Day 10

Forgiving One Another

Reflect: Col. 3:12-13; Eph. 4:31-32; Mk. 11:25-26; Jn. 20:22-23

Repent: Of harboring unforgiveness and resentments against family members; of allowing petty disagreements to disrupt family unity, love, and joy; of not quickly demonstrating forgiveness toward one another; of tolerating and excusing unforgiveness in ourselves; of not intentionally and consistently training our children in the way of forgiveness; of _____

_____

Receive: Forgiveness, as you forgive others, remembering that Jesus taught that "If you forgive men when they sin against you, your heavenly Father will also forgive you. But if you do not forgive men their sins, your Father will not forgive your sins" (Mt. 6:14-15).

Revive: Pray for forgiveness to permeate families throughout the church, that our families would be free from the destructive power of unforgiveness and the damage that comes from harboring past hurt or resentment; that love would be released to cover a multitude of sins within families so restoration and healthy relationships might abound.

Rejoice: That our God is a forgiving God and that He desires to give us His grace to forgive, just as we have been forgiven; that His mercies are new every morning; that by His Spirit He enables us to walk in new ways of grace, mercy, and love by demonstrating forgiveness to one another.

Day 11

Disciplining in Love and the Fear of the Lord

Reflect: Prov. 22:6; Eph. 6:4; Col. 3:21; 2 Tim. 3:15

Repent: Of disciplining children in harshness and anger rather than in love; of provoking our children to wrath through unrealistic expectations, legalistic regulations, or motivations rooted in pride, selfishness, or personal preferences; of not training children in the way they should go to fulfill God's purposes for them; of inconsistency in the discipline of children; of using secular models of discipline rather than God's Word; of _____

_____

Receive: Forgiveness and the instruction of the Lord to begin disciplining and training children in His ways, His Word, and His purposes; a fresh revelation of the fear of the Lord that can be imparted to our children in love and holiness.

Revive: Pray that a revival of godly parenting would permeate the church, restoring God's divine order of love and holiness within the family unit; that parents would be set free from unholy and unhealthy ways of discipline that provoke children to wrath rather than godliness and self-control; that love would rule over all areas of discipline, training, and instruction in our homes; that the Word of God would be recognized as the standard and motivation of all training in Christian homes.

Rejoice: That God disciplines us as a good Father and He has set forth principles of training and discipline in His Word; that He is well able and willing to teach us, as parents, how to lead our children; that He loves to answer prayer regarding our children and has given us many promises for His loving care over them.

Day 12

Obeying and Honoring Parents

Reflect: Ex. 20:12; Dt. 5:16,33; Mt. 15:1-9; Col. 3:20; Eph. 6:1-3

Repent: Of all disobedience and dishonoring of parents, present or past (ask the Lord if you need to go to your parents to ask forgiveness for past sins); of attitudes that dishonor parents in word or in deed; of unforgiveness that gives way to dishonor and rebellion against parents (and other God-ordained people of authority); of neglecting to honor aging parents and/or generations past through actions, words, or attitudes; of tolerating disobedience and disrespect from our children; of _____

_____

Receive: Forgiveness and grace to begin walking in a new way toward parents—whether as a child in the home or as an adult with aging parents. Ask the Lord to reveal ways to intentionally demonstrate honor to your parents.

Revive: Intercede for obedience and honor to return to our homes. Pray that children of all ages would be taught the importance and significance of learning and living in obedience; that parents would be diligent in disciplining children with love so they can live in obedience and honor; that children would learn obedience to parents that will mature into faithful obedience to the Lord and His ordained authorities throughout their lives.

Rejoice: That Jesus learned obedience through the things He suffered to be an example to us; that God has granted us earthly parents to lovingly teach us to obey, so that our lives may be blessed.

Day 13

Studying God's Word and Praying Together

Reflect: Dt. 6:6-9, 11:18-21; 2 Tim. 3:15-17; Eph. 6:18

Repent: Of failing diligently to teach our children the Scriptures and the ways of the Lord; of depending on others to train and teach our children God's Word; of neglecting the discipline and privilege of praying together; of failing to pray for each other that the purposes of God might be fulfilled; of _____
_____
_____

Receive: Forgiveness and a renewed hunger for God's Word and fresh ways of studying His Word as a family.

Revive: Pray for insight and revelation from the Holy Spirit to be given to all members of the family; a return to talking with our children about God's Word throughout the day; for a desire for prayer to be stirred up within all family members and that answers to prayer would come to encourage faith and consistency; that the world would see evidence of God's working in and through our families by His Word and prayer.

Rejoice: That God desires all of us to lift up holy hands in prayer and that He promises to answer those who call upon His name; that He will give the Spirit of revelation and truth as we seek His face.

Day 14

Honoring One Another in Love

Reflect: Rom. 12:9-13; Phil. 2:1-4

Repent: Of not honoring and preferring family members and others who are in close relationship with us; of thinking more highly of ourselves than we ought; of resisting opportunities to yield our own preferences to those of the Lord, as revealed through others in our families or in the church; of being unwilling to honor others in humility and love; of

_____

_____

Receive: Forgiveness and grace to honor and give preference to our families and close relationships.

Revive: Pray that a spirit of humility would permeate our families, releasing us to honor and prefer one another, particularly in difficult times; that holy honor for spouses, parents, and children would be restored in our speech, attitudes, and actions; that loving concern for one another would outweigh selfish desires.

Rejoice: That Jesus Christ came to earth and set forth a holy example of living in humility, honoring His earthly father and mother, and honoring His heavenly Father; that He has given us His Holy Spirit to enable us to live in love, honor, and humility.

SECTION 3

Our Relationship with Our Local Congregation

The Lord, in His grace and mercy, ordained that we be fitly joined to other believers of like mind, passion, and purpose. One of the foundational expressions of body life is found within the local congregation. In this place we learn to function together as the body of Christ—worshiping, working, serving, and loving as one. In this context, God has provided a safe place for us to grow in maturity of character, exercise our spiritual gifts, and practice serving the Lord with gladness.

This week,

pray for your local congregation, other congregations in our city, and for all believers to come into God's revealed plan of fellowship and order for believers— to touch the world with His love.

Day 15

Walking under Authority

Reflect: Mt. 8:5-13, 28:18-20; Ro. 13:1-7; 1 Pet. 5:1-11

Repent: Of ways in which godly authority has been rejected or dishonored; of presuming too much personal authority without proper relationship to God's prescribed order of authority within the church; of criticizing and speaking evil of church leadership, especially pastors; of failing to faithfully pray for those in authority; of _____
_____

Receive: Forgiveness and grace to walk with all humility, honor, and joy in proper relationship to those who are in authority over us; an increase of kingdom authority as we walk in God's divine order.

Revive: Pray for God's divine order to be established in righteousness, truth, and justice within the church, both in our local congregation and the churches within our city; for God to raise up men and women of integrity, faith, and love to places of spiritual authority throughout the city; for a revival of God's governmental order in His church, that He might teach us His way and His will.

Rejoice: That God is our ultimate authority and in His sovereignty He has established those whom He has purposed to be in authority over our lives; that He knows what we need and that what He establishes is and will be for our good, to the praise and glory of His holy name.

Day 16

Walking in Authority

Reflect: Lk. 9:1-6, 10:1-12; Acts 1:8; 2 Cor. 12:9-10, 13:10

Repent: Of walking in self-proclaimed or self-exerted authority rather than in the authority that comes only in the name of the Lord Jesus Christ and according to His apportionment by grace; of walking in the world's expression of authority rather than in God's way of humility, servanthood, and submission; of trusting in personal authority and power rather than in the the power that works within us through the Holy Spirit; of presuming authority beyond the measure entrusted to us by the Lord and confirmed through those in authority over us; of _____

_____

Receive: Forgiveness and understanding of God's revealed divine order and provision for walking in authority, first under His authority and then, under those whose care He has positioned us for His purposes.

Revive: Pray for a revival that will properly position God's people under His authority and those He has appointed; for a release of godly authority in all believers to walk victoriously over the assaults of the enemy, demonstrating His power and grace to the lost in our city; for a baptism of authority wed with Christlike character that will encourage and edify others, not cause destruction or discouragement.

Rejoice: That Christ is the perfect example and provision for walking in authority; that to walk under authority releases the proper authority that Jesus referred to as being of great faith (Mt. 8:5-13).

Day 17

Walking Together in Love

Reflect: Ro. 12:9-21; 1 Tim. 1:5-11; 1 Pet. 4:7-11

Repent: Of the times when love has not been the motivation behind the actions, attitudes, or words spoken within the fellowship of believers; of ways that love for others has not ruled in our heart through Christ Jesus; of actions that have defied words of love; of loving hypocritically; of _____

_____

Receive: A fresh revelation of God's love that cleanses us from all unrighteousness and floods the soul with the amazing joy, peace, and love of His presence; a fresh love for others that is birthed in the love of God.

Revive: Pray that the church would walk in love for one another, taking up the admonitions of Scripture to love fervently, without hypocrisy, and out of a pure heart; for the love of Christ to permeate His church so that the world would see and believe that God loves them and sent His Son so that they might live in His love through salvation.

Rejoice: That we can love because He first loved us; that Christ pours out His love on us, in us, and through us; that love is not something we must conjure up by our own strength, but is a gift of grace that we choose to walk in by His Spirit.

Day 18

Walking Together in Unity

Reflect: Psalm 133; John 17; Eph. 4:1-6

Repent: Of the many things that have allowed division, dissension, and disagreement to keep us from walking together as the body of Christ; of harboring judgments, prejudices, and prideful attitudes toward fellow believers; of disregarding the words of Scripture to walk in unity with one another; of

_____

_____

Receive: Forgiveness and a fresh filling of the Holy Spirit to enable and empower us to walk in the unity of the Spirit in the bond of peace.

Revive: Pray that congregations all over our city would grow in unity of the Spirit, love, peace, purpose, and passion—so that the world might see the power and grace of God manifested in diversity coming together in the love of Christ; that petty differences, pride, selfish ambitions, etc., would be laid down for the sake of reflecting the purposes and character of Christ.

Rejoice: That God is able to accomplish that which His church needs; that Jesus' prayer in John 17 is a top priority in the heart of God—He longs to see the full answer manifested on the earth as it is in heaven.

Day 19

Walking Together in the Body

Reflect: Ro. 12:3-8; 1 Corinthians 12; Eph. 4:7-16

Repent: Of not accepting, honoring, or joining together with the various parts of the body—particularly those God has joined us to through the local congregation; of withholding fellowship from those that are unlike you in personality, ethnic origin, or gifting; of not working and ministering alongside others within the body of Christ, thereby blocking "every joint from supplying what is needful for growth and edification of the body"; of _____

_____

_____

Receive: The washing of the water of the Word to cleanse all sin and defilement of the flesh; a fresh understanding of God's value of the body through His Word.

Revive: Pray for every member of the body of Christ to discover our place and come into proper relationship with the other members, first within the local congregation and then beyond; for each member to walk faithfully in God's gifting and calling to build up others; that the fullness of Christ's life might be expressed freely through the body, properly functioning together in love.

Rejoice: That it is the will of the Father for the church to function together as the body of Christ; that we can pray these prayers with confidence that they are His will in the name of Jesus.

Day 20

Walking Together in God's Vision

Reflect: Acts 11:19-26, 13:1-3 (Antioch), Acts 19:1-41 (Ephesus) These two churches are examples that local congregations and cities have unique purposes in God to fulfill. The same is true in our day, and it is imperative that we walk together in God's revealed vision for local congregations within our city.

Repent: Of ways in which we have resisted or rejected the stated vision for our local congregation; of operating in ways that contradict the accepted revelation of God's purposes for our local congregation; of failing to know God's specific vision for our local congregation; of _____
_____

Receive: Restoration in areas where disunity or confusion of vision has caused problems; hope for walking together in God's appointed vision to reach our community with the love of Christ.

Revive: Pray that each congregation would be led into the place of discovering, embracing, and pursuing God's vision; that members of the body would cooperate with local leadership in this process; that God would supply all the necessary members to fulfill His vision; that members of the congregation would walk together in love, unity, and purpose to fulfill God's will.

Rejoice: That God has a vision for each congregation that fits within His purposes for their city, region, and nation; that He desires to reveal His vision and His will to us and that this is for our good and the advancement of His kingdom.

Day 21

Pursuing God Together

Reflect: Hos. 6:1-3; 1 Pet. 3:8-12; Heb. 10:19-25

Repent: Of any ways in which seeking the Lord together as an assembly of believers has been forsaken or disregarded; of failing to recognize and walk in the value Scripture places on relationship and fellowship in pursuing God together; of any lack of faith for believing that when we pursue God He will meet us; of _____

_____

Receive: Fresh love and desire for fellowship with other believers; grace to walk together in pursuit of the Lord, humbly learning and receiving from one another in love; a divine fit from the Lord into the body of believers He has joined you to.

Revive: Pray for humility and passion to permeate local congregations all across our city, uniting us in pursuit of the Lord and releasing revival fire; for pastors and church leaders to lead congregations with love and meekness to seek the Lord in one accord; that faith will arise among God's children for revival in our day.

Rejoice: That it is God's desire to revive His church and to have a people prepared in unity for His return; that it is His will that His people would so demonstrate His purity, passion, and power that the world would seek Him and be saved.

SECTION 4

Our Relationship with the Church in Our City

Another sphere of our love relationships is among our brothers and sisters in the broader body of Christ. Too often, we do not live in love, respect, and unity with one another. We have allowed disagreements, misunderstandings, false doctrine, and destructive devices of the enemy to divide and distort what God intended to be His church, meeting in many different congregations, in a city. Christ has one bride—and we must come to a place of living and loving in the unity of the Spirit in the bond of peace.

This week,

let the high priestly prayer of Jesus Christ—that we might be one—undergird our prayers. The world is looking for the church to rise together as one in the Spirit through Christ Jesus our Lord.

Day 22

Pursuing Unity and Cooperation

Reflect: Jn. 17:20-26; Psalm 133; Gal. 3:26-29; Eph. 2:14-22, 4:1-6

Repent: Of operating in disunity, isolation, separation, and division toward followers of Christ who do not attend our own congregation or who have differences of belief on the non-essentials of the faith; of criticizing and judging other congregations or denominations; of allowing things that were never intended to unite us to divide us; of allowing pride, hard-heartedness, or an unteachable spirit to keep us from working together in the unity of the Spirit in the bond of peace; of _____

_____

Receive: Forgiveness and the appropriation of Christ's finished work on the cross that tore down the wall of division; divine enablement to walk in unity and cooperation with believers throughout the city and world.

Revive: Intercede for the body of Christ to function according to Christ's finished work on the cross—in love, unity, harmony, and humility; for individuals and congregations to begin pursuing unity and cooperation with other believing congregations in their areas; for hunger to arise in God's people for one another, bringing congregations together for the advancement of the kingdom of God (to see many come to faith in Christ).

Rejoice: That this was Christ's prayer for us prior to the cross, and it remains the desire of the Godhead to see the church—His body, His bride—living, loving, and working together as one, even as He is one. Rejoice that this prayer will be answered because it is clearly the will of the Father, Son, and Holy Spirit.

Day 23

Pursuing Wisdom and Understanding Together

Reflect: Ps. 119:33-40; Prov. 2:1-11, 3:5-6; Is. 11:2-5; Jas. 1:2-8, 3:13-17

Repent: Of trusting in our own understanding or not pursuing the understanding and wisdom that comes only from the Lord; of discounting or discrediting the wisdom and understanding others in the body of Christ have gleaned from seeking the Lord; of being fearful or hesitant in seeking the Lord with others in the broader body of Christ; of failing to trust the Lord to give wisdom and understanding to all those who seek Him; of failing to trust the Lord to protect us from counterfeit expressions of wisdom and understanding; of

_____

_____

Receive: Forgiveness and the provision of wisdom and understanding that God promises to those who earnestly ask Him; a fresh filling of the Holy Spirit for wisdom, understanding, counsel, might, knowledge, and the fear of the Lord, which is the beginning of wisdom.

Revive: Pray for the church to increase in pursuit of God's wisdom and understanding; to be set free from the tyranny of the world's system of understanding; for a revival of the fear of the Lord to permeate the church worldwide; that as believers, we would lay down our own ways for the ways of the Lord; for an increase in our hunger for the Word of God and for wise teachers to lead us into the Lord's wisdom and understanding, which leads to life.

Rejoice: That God has promised to give wisdom to those who ask; that the Holy Spirit is the Spirit of wisdom and revelation; that He reveals truth to our hearts as we seek the Lord and will continue to lead us into the depths of the wisdom and riches of the Lord Jesus Christ.

Day 24

Pursuing Reconciliation in Truth and Love

Reflect: 2 Cor. 5:12-21; Eph. 2:16-18; Col. 1:19-23
Definition: *Reconcile*—to change, exchange, reestablish, restore relationship, make things right, remove an enmity. Describes the re-establishing of a proper, loving, interpersonal relationship, which has been broken or disrupted. (from "Word Wealth," *The Spirit-Filled Life Bible*, Nelson Publishers, 1991).

Repent: Of not being properly reconciled to the Lord and to His children; of allowing disagreements, arguments, and vain pursuits to keep you separated from others in the body of Christ; of not submitting to the Spirit of truth and love; of not submitting to the compelling love of Christ to be reconciled to one another; of _____
_____

Receive: The gift of reconciliation from the Lord through repentance, being restored into a deeper level of loving intimacy with Him; grace and love to be reconciled to those with whom we have been estranged.

Revive: Pray for believers throughout our city to be burdened with Christ's compelling love to be reconciled to one another; for truth and love to cause individuals and congregations throughout the city to pursue reconciliation with those from whom they are separated or with whom they have suffered a break in relationship; that the enemy of unity who works division by accusing brother against brother would be defeated by the power of love permeating throughout the church in this day.

Rejoice: That He who is in us is greater than he that is in the world; that the Lord desires that we be reconciled and come together in truth and love; that He makes us one by His Spirit through love and truth.

Day 25

Pursuing Genuine Relationships through Fellowship

Reflect: Acts 2:42-47; Gal. 2:1-10; Phil. 2:1-4; 1 Jn. 1:1-10

Repent: Of failing to pursue genuine relationships with fellow believers; of living in separation and isolation from believers within our communities or families because of petty differences of belief; of declaring love for God while not living in love with brothers and sisters in the Lord; of _____

_____

Receive: Forgiveness and a fresh baptism of love for the family of God; a fresh desire to embrace fellowship and communion with others who follow Jesus Christ as Savior and Lord.

Revive: Intercede for the body of Christ to return to the ways of the early church in continuing steadfastly in the apostles' teaching and fellowship, in the breaking of bread, and in prayer; for a fresh conviction and commitment that brings the church to pursue genuine relationships with those who are different from ourselves in culture, race, ethnicity, socio-economics, history, or any other area of distinction; for the church to find ways to intentionally and significantly grow together in fellowship and relationship.

Rejoice: That God is a God of fellowship and communion and, as a good Father, He loves to draw His children together; that we have one Father who has blessed us with the beauty of diversity.

Day 26

Pursuing Forgiveness and Humility Together

Reflect: Mt. 6:14-15, 18:1-35; Eph. 4:25-32; Col. 3:12-17; 1 Pet. 5:5-11

Repent: Of not forgiving those who have sinned against us; of walking in pride, superiority, or opposition to others in the body of Christ; of not walking in tenderness, humility, kindness, meekness, longsuffering, or forgiveness toward one another; of failing to submit to God and resist the devil, especially with regard to walking in the unity of Christ's Spirit; of

_____

_____

Receive: Forgiveness, once we have forgiven; restoration of things lost through unforgiveness and pride; fresh grace to walk in forgiveness and humility toward others.

Revive: Intercede for the church to practice forgiveness, demonstrating the amazing grace we each have received in Christ Jesus our Lord; for true humility to permeate the church and that the enemy's counterfeit humility, which keeps people bound, will be driven out of the church in the name of the Lord Jesus Christ; for the church to be cloaked in a garment of humility and grace so that Christ is increasingly revealed through her to the world.

Rejoice: That we have been granted much forgiveness and the grace to forgive, even as we have been forgiven; that God's desire is for His church to walk in the power of love through forgiveness and humility.

Day 27

Pursuing Ministry and Service Together

Reflect: Romans 12; 1 Corinthians 12; Eph. 4:7-16

Repent: Of not valuing others and their God-given gifts, talents, and abilities; of operating in independence rather than in God's ordained order of interdependence of the body; of despising spiritual gifts that we fear or don't understand; of wrongfully judging others within the body (for pride, error, perceived lack of value, etc.); of not functioning as a "whole body, joined and held together by every supporting ligament," which "grows and builds itself up in love" (Eph. 4:16); of

_____

_____

Receive: God's cleansing power to restore and revive us in relationship with others in the body of Christ; fresh revelation of the body of Christ as one new people and the bride of Christ.

Revive: Pray for the church to be awakened to the wonder of being joined as one by the Spirit of the Lord; that we will all learn to value and esteem every part of the body, seen and unseen; that we learn to submit to God's divine order for His church; that grace to minister and serve together in love, honor, and humility will permeate the church.

Rejoice: That Christ set His church in order when He ascended; that He delights to answer our prayers that we might be one on earth, reflecting the spiritual reality of heaven.

Day 28

Pursuing Worship—Together

Reflect: 2 Chron. 5:2-14; Psalm 95, 150; Jn. 4:21-26; Rev. 4:1-11

Repent: Of failing to worship the Lord without division; of not worshiping according to the patterns set by the Lord in Scripture; of judging expressions or styles of worship as more important than the heart of worship; of failing to cultivate an atmosphere of worship that honors the Father, glorifies Christ, and welcomes the Holy Spirit in corporate gatherings; of _____

_____

Receive: Forgiveness and a fresh baptism of the love of Christ that stirs us to worship in spirit and truth; of a desire, born of the Spirit, to worship with others who love the Lord Jesus Christ—regardless of style, personal preference, or anything else the enemy would use to divide us from one another.

Revive: Intercede for a release of fresh passion for worship among all God's children; for the walls of division created by personal preferences, style, judgment, or anything else to be brought down; for the various streams (expressions and practices) of the church to come together for times of corporate worship; for the church, locally and corporately, to create a place where the Holy Spirit would be welcomed in the midst of worship.

Rejoice: That God promises in His Word to inhabit the praises of His people (Ps. 22:3) and to be in their midst where two or three are gathered together in His name; that He is sending forth a fresh wind of His Spirit upon His church to worship together in spirit and in truth.

SECTION 5

Our Relationship with the World

Jesus said in Jn. 3:17 that He did not come to condemn the world, but that through Him the world might be saved. He did not take His followers out of the world, but rather left us in the world to live as a demonstration and testimony of His saving grace, mercy, truth, and love, so that the world might be saved through Him. Our purpose on the earth is to glorify the Lord, and He is most glorified as others come to know Jesus Christ as Savior and Lord.

Therefore, this week,
as we press on in these forty days of repentance and prayer,
we focus on the world and our relationship to those
who do not yet know Jesus Christ personally. Invite
the Holy Spirit to search your heart and to reveal areas
where transformation needs to occur in you
and in the church, so that the world may see Christ more
clearly and come to a saving knowledge of Him.

Day 29

Demonstrating the Love of Christ

Reflect: Jn. 3:1-21, 17:6-19; 1 Jn. 3:1-23

Repent: Of declaring that we love when demonstrating lack of love and concern for those who are lost without Christ; of speaking love, but not showing love through deeds that touch the lives of those in the world around us; of demonstrating the letter of the law rather than the Spirit of liberty and love; of failing to live as Christ lived, in the world, but not of it; of

_____

_____

Receive: A new impartation of holy love for the world, just as Christ loved the world and gave His life for it; a fresh grace to demonstrate the love of Christ in tangible ways to those in our community who do not know Christ.

Revive: Pray for the church to be a living, vital force of love in the earth today; that we will be known by our love for one another and the loving-kindness of the Lord that leads to repentance for the lost; for the church to birth new and creative ways to show the world love that is genuine, significant, and relevant; for the church to be delivered from legalism and released into the liberty of the Spirit.

Rejoice: That Christ first loved us, so we can love by His grace; that Christ's love overcomes evil, does not rejoice in evil, casts out fear, and covers a multitude of sin.

Day 30

Demonstrating God's Grace

Reflect: Jn. 1:14-18; Acts 4:32-33, 11:19-24, 14:1-7,21-28; 1 Pet. 4:7-11

Repent: Of receiving grace but not demonstrating grace to others; of limiting our understanding of grace to conversion alone, ignoring the divine enablement of grace that He gives us to live a life of testimony that glorifies Him; of testing the Lord and not trusting Him fully through daily obedience; of

_____

_____

Receive: Fresh grace to live according to His commands and His call upon our lives; His grace (divine favor) to be and to do all that He requires of us in these days.

Revive: Pray for the church to receive a fresh revelation of the marvelous grace of the Lord Jesus Christ; to have faith to live graciously toward those in our communities who do not yet know Christ; to see grace as a gift we have received and are to bestow freely upon others; that a restoration of graciousness in our attitude, speech, and actions will permeate the church and touch the world.

Rejoice: That God is a gracious God, full of compassion and abounding in mercy; that we are recipients of His saving, redeeming, delivering grace.

Day 31

Demonstrating Mercy, Loving-kindness, and Goodness

Reflect: Lam. 3:22-33; Ro. 2:1-16, 9:14-29; Gal. 5:22-23

Repent: Of failing to show acts of kindness to those who mistreat or revile us or our loved ones; of withholding mercy out of judgment, loving-kindness out of vengeance, or goodness out of so-called "righteous" indignation; of demonstrating a counterfeit mercy that does not line up with God's truth, righteousness, and holy love; of _____
_____

Receive: Forgiveness and grace to walk in ways that reveal the holiness of God's mercy, loving-kindness, and goodness.

Revive: Intercede for the church to grow in grace, mercy, and love to impact the world; that the fruit of the Spirit would abound in and through the church; that God's pruning of His church would bring forth a bountiful harvest through demonstrations of goodness that lead many to repentance and salvation; that the church would be known for her mercy, love, and goodness, pointing to the Lord Jesus Christ with clarity and power.

Rejoice: That the Lord Jesus Christ sent His Holy Spirit to fill us and enable us to walk in His life of mercy and to demonstrate loving-kindness and goodness; that what He has called us to do, He enables us to do by His grace.

Day 32

Demonstrating Truth in Love

Reflect: Ps. 85:8-13; Zech. 8:16-17; Jn. 8:31-36; Eph. 4:15

Repent: Of not living in truth or demonstrating truth in love; of using truth as a weapon that wounds rather than as a revelation that sets people free; of telling truth without love saturating every expression; of telling people the truth without loving them first; of _____

_____

Receive: Forgiveness and revelation of the love of God in His truth; an understanding that truth without love is not a true reflection of the Lord God Almighty.

Revive: Pray that the church would come to a greater understanding and demonstration of truth in love; that the Holy Spirit would release new ways to demonstrate truth to the world in ways that would draw unbelievers to faith; that truth would increase to, in, and through us, bringing liberty to all who hear.

Rejoice: That Jesus is the Way, the Truth, and the Life; that through Him salvation is available to all who will believe; that He declared that we shall know the truth and the truth shall set us free.

Day 33

Demonstrating the Life of the Spirit

Reflect: Ro. 8:12-14; Eph. 5:15-21

Repent: Of living according to the flesh and its desires rather than the Spirit of love; of failing to demonstrate the fruit of the Spirit, especially to those who do not yet know Christ as Savior and Lord; of failing to recognize the Lord's work in your life by lack of faith in and surrender to His Word and Holy Spirit; of _____

_____

Receive: Forgiveness and restoration by the power of the Holy Spirit to live in the Spirit and not in the flesh; fresh hope for living in a new way that will more clearly reveal Christ to the world.

Revive: Intercede for all believers to walk as sons of God, led by the Spirit of God toward increasing maturity; to grow in faith and surrender to the Holy Spirit as a powerful demonstration of His love and power; to walk in the fullness of Christ's grace as members of the body of Christ, demonstrating His love, mercy, grace, and power to the world.

Rejoice: That the Holy Spirit lives within us, enabling and empowering us to walk according to the ways of Christ; that it is not by power or might but by the Spirit of the Lord that we demonstrate His life to the world.

Day 34

Demonstrating the Ministry of Reconciliation

Reflect: Mt. 5:21-26; Eph. 2:14-18; 1 Tim. 6:11-19; 1 Pet. 3:8-17

Repent: Of not pursuing righteousness, godliness, faith, love, patience, gentleness, and peace, particularly with those who do not yet know Christ as Savior; of not responding to wrong treatment or suffering with righteousness and goodness; of not being intentional in reconciling with those from whom we are separated; of _____

_____

_____

Receive: Forgiveness for sins of commission and sins of omission; grace to begin pursuing attitudes, words, and actions of reconciliation with our community.

Revive: Pray for the church to submit to the Holy Spirit, seeking to demonstrate abundantly the fruit of the Spirit to the world around us; for tangible expressions of reconciliation to prevail in and through the church; for the reconciliation we have in Christ to compel us to share the gospel of Christ with the lost, so that they too might be reconciled to God; for grace and patience to flow through believers to the lost, especially for believers who have been mistreated, criticized, or persecuted for righteousness' sake.

Rejoice: That the love of Christ compels us; that the Holy Spirit empowers us to care for and reach out to the world with the ministry of reconciliation; that we don't have to, nor can we, do this by our own strength; that He who calls us to this ministry will enable us to fulfill it for His glory.

Day 35

Demonstrating the Servant-heart of Christ

Reflect: Mt. 20:20-28; Jn. 13:1-17; Phil. 2:5-18

Repent: Of not walking in the attitude of Christ Jesus who came to serve, not to be served; of failing to serve others; of expecting to be served by others, demonstrating pride rather than humility; of selectively choosing whom we serve by personal preferences, not by a motivation to demonstrate Christ's love through service; of _____

_____

Receive: Forgiveness and a revival of spirit to walk in the ways of Christ in service, humility, and reverence.

Revive: Pray for the church to learn how to serve as Christ did, demonstrating God's *agape* love; to discover ways of serving our communities that will soften the hearts of unbelievers to the gospel of love, life, and truth; to be clothed in humility in order to serve out of the love Christ has bestowed upon us; to remember that without the grace of God we all would be facing an eternity without Christ; that our service would be a holy demonstration of Christ's love, not self-serving in any way; that the world would receive our service as a demonstration of Christ's love for them, leading many to salvation; that holy reverance for God would motivate us to serve others with love.

Rejoice: That Christ Jesus came to serve and not to be served; that we can reflect His character by serving others in grateful response; that through such services as worship, preaching the gospel, and building the church, Christ advances His kingdom on earth.

SECTION 6
Our Ongoing Pursuit of God

The hope of revival leads us to draw near to God as the bride of Christ—in unity of faith, purpose, and expectation. Scripture resounds with evidence of what God does when His people come together in humility to seek His face, hear His voice, and follow His ways. As these forty days of repentance, fasting, and prayer draw to an end, we have taken another step in our pursuit of God. It is neither the first step, nor the last. We must consecrate ourselves to press onward in our quest for revival—for transformation—in our city, ushering thousands into the kingdom of God through faith in Christ Jesus our Lord.

During these last five days,

let us consecrate to humble ourselves and pray, seek His face, and turn from our wicked ways, that He might hear from heaven, forgive our sins, and heal our land (2 Chron. 7:14). May the church in our city be rallied together to transform our city with the presence of Christ—for His glory and honor alone.

Day 36

Living a Life of Humility and Repentance

Reflect: 2 Chron. 7:12-22, 29:3-19; Jer. 4:1-18; Joel 2:12-32; Mt. 3:2; Acts 2:38-39

Repent: Of any attempts toward revival without humility and consistency in turning toward the Lord; of allowing an attitude of "done that already" to penetrate our daily living; of resisting God's call to humility and repentance out of pride or hardness of heart; of wrongly thinking that revival is a call for others and not myself or my local congregation; of

_____

_____

Receive: Forgiveness and a fresh impartation of God's grace to live a life of humility and repentance.

Revive: Pray that the church in our city would be overwhelmed with a spirit of humility and repentance, turning from the ways of the world and toward the Lord; that the number of believers following the ways of humility and repentance would increase exponentially; that the promise of revival would be poured out upon the people of God as we walk in His ways; that the grace of God would impact the world through us as we follow Him in humble obedience.

Rejoice: That God has promised to revive and refresh those who humble themselves and turn to Him with all their hearts; that God's promises are "Yes" and "Amen" in Christ Jesus our Lord.

Day 37

Living a Life of Prayer and Intercession

Reflect: 1 Sam. 12:20-25; Isaiah 56, 62; Ro. 8:26-30; Eph. 6:10-18; Phil. 4:4-9

Repent: Of failing to pray or growing weary or sluggish in persevering in prayer; of departing from the call to watch and pray as watchmen on the wall of our city; of not yielding to the Holy Spirit who makes intercession through us; of not being joyful, grateful, and hopeful in our prayers; of not pursuing becoming a house of prayer for all nations; of _____
_____
_____

Receive: Forgiveness and the spirit of grace and supplication to embark upon a life of prayer and intercession; faith that we will see Christ rule and reign in the hearts of men, women, boys, and girls in our city.

Revive: Ask that prayer and intercession will increase in purity, passion, and power throughout our city; that those called to mobilize, lead, and encourage others in prayer will be raised up, trained, and equipped throughout the church; that a fresh baptism of the Holy Spirit would come upon every prayer meeting in the city, bringing forth prayers that are in agreement with Jesus Christ and pleasing to the Father until He answers with revival fire from heaven; that our city will be transformed by the presence of Christ as we cry out in humble and faith-filled intercession.

Rejoice: That God has established that His church will be called a house of prayer for all nations and that His people will be joyful in His house of prayer; that He gives joy to those who faithfully seek His face in prayer with thanksgiving and faith.

Day 38

Listening to His Voice

Reflect: Ps. 81:8-16; Jer. 7:23-27, 23:26; Jn. 10:22-30

Repent: Of not heeding the voice of the Lord; of allowing fear, doubt, or unbelief to hinder our willingness and ability to hear the voice of our Good Shepherd; of hearing but not obeying His voice; of trusting in the voice of others more than in the voice of the Lord; of mocking those who openly confess and testify to listening and hearing His voice; of

_____

_____

Receive: Forgiveness and fresh assurance of being able to hear as God's children, the sheep of His pasture; the gift of ears to hear what the Sprit is saying to the church today (Rev. 2:7).

Revive: Intercede for the church to come to a place of being quiet before the Lord, expecting to hear what He has to speak today; for grace to walk in humble obedience to His voice; for ears to hear from the Lord in the way He has chosen to speak to and through His children; that a deepening desire to hear His voice more clearly will permeate the church.

Rejoice: That our God is a communicating God who loves to speak with His children in words of love, affirmation, correction, direction, instruction, tenderness, strength, encouragement, edification, and comfort; that He continues to speak—even when we turn a deaf ear—and that He continues to woo us back to Himself.

Day 39

Exalting His Name

Reflect: Ex. 15:1-2; Ps. 34:1-3, Psalm 99; Phil. 2:5-11

Repent: Of not magnifying and lifting high the name and person of Jesus Christ; of exalting anyone other than Christ; of not faithfully participating in praise and worship of the Lord—personally and corporately; of not giving the Lord the honor that is due His name; of _____

_____

Receive: Forgiveness for misplaced honor, praise, or attention; restoration of a heart of praise and worship which lifts Christ high, far above all others.

Revive: Pray for the church to have a fuller, more biblical understanding of the majesty and glory of the Lord Jesus Christ; to see Him for who He is—King of kings, Lord of lords, Sovereign Lord of all, Holy and Majestic One—and that there is none like Him in heaven or on the earth.

Rejoice: That He is the Exalted One and that will never change; that He gives us the privilege of celebrating and honoring His rightful place as the Almighty Lord; that His name is above every name, and that at His name every knee will bow and every tongue confess that Jesus Christ is Lord to the glory of God the Father. Hallelujah!

Day 40

Worshiping God—Together, Forever

Reflect: 1 Chron. 16:7-36; Psalms 95, 96; Jn. 4:21-26

Repent: Of failure to humble oneself before the Lord, acknowledging His total lordship; of not gathering with other believers to worship the Lord in spirit and in truth; of not giving our all to the Lord as an act of worship; of worshiping in form without the substance of the heart; of _____

_____

_____

Receive: Forgiveness and a heart revived to passionately and completely worship the Lord, simply because He is worthy of all our praise, worship, and adoration.

Revive: Pray for the church to have a Christ-centered experience of worship in spirit and truth that will please the Father; for legitimate and honest exaltation of the name of the Lord, born of the Holy Spirit and the Word; for humility and unity among believers that will give rise to worshiping the Lord in the beauty of His holiness throughout His church.

Rejoice: That the Word of God declares that the day has come when the Lord is worshiped in spirit and in truth throughout the world; that He deserves and demands our worship; that our God reigns now and forever. Amen!

Closing Thoughts

These forty days have been but one phase of a journey that has gone on for years and will undoubtedly continue for years after us—until Jesus returns for His church, His bride. The issues of repentance and intercession seem to be endless. Fortunately, we have a God who asks only that we join Him in faithful obedience to what He reveals each day through His Word and by His Holy Spirit. He intercedes for us continually that these purposes might be fulfilled in our lives.

Remember that God loves us more than we can imagine and He desires to bring revival to our city—even more than we want it! He knows what we need, far more than we do. He is able to do—exceedingly, abundantly—more than we could ever ask for or think of. He is simply waiting for us to respond to Him in repentance, humility, brokenness, and unity, and to ask by faith for what we need—*MORE OF JESUS!*

Father, hear our prayers, touch our lives, transform us by Your grace to be more like Your Son, Jesus. Do whatever You must do in and through us, to fulfill Your desire to see our city transformed by Your presence. Prepare us, O Lord, to walk in humility, grace, mercy, love, and power so that the world might see and know that Jesus Christ is Lord, and that they might come to salvation through His precious name. Father, we trust You and wait patiently on You, earnestly desiring to see Your kingdom come on earth—in our city—as it is in heaven. In Jesus' name we ask. Amen and Amen.

What to Do Now

Congratulations! You have completed this prayer initiative. God has probably placed a greater hunger for Himself within you. But you may be thinking, what do I do now? You want to continue to grow in your renewed relationship with Jesus. You want to encourage others in their faith as well. Here are several action steps to consider. Ask God to direct you in what He would have you do.

Personal Life

To continue growing in your personal relationship with God, you need to be both proactive and sit back and relax!

Be proactive by determining to spend time with God each day. Keep reading His Word and meditating on it. Pray through it. If this devotional prayer guide helped you, find others to enhance your times with Him. *The Jabez Prayer Guide* by Jacquie Tyre is a great place to start.

Sit back and relax by letting God do the major work in you.

1. Ask Him to give you a hunger for Himself. Make this a continuous prayer. Watch what He does!

2. Surrender to Him daily. We often take back control of our will. We need to regularly surrender our will to His will.

3. Ask the Holy Spirit to fill you. D.L. Moody was once asked why he prayed so often for the Holy Spirit's filling in his life. "Because I leak," he responded.

Helping Others

If you want to be a catalyst for revival in the lives of others, there are also some things you can do.

1. Pray through this guide with your church or small group. If you did this initiative by yourself, why not do it again with others. Watch what God does in the life of your church as you seek His fullness together.

2. Study other available literature on revival. Don't let a hunger for revival wane. There are many other products available for both individual or group study. *Pray!* has released two additional products on revival that lend themselves to group study:

An Urgent Appeal. Produced by the National Revival Network, *An Urgent Appeal* is a 64-page booklet, complete with questions, designed to stimulate discussion on revival. Go to www.urgentappeal.net for more information on this material or to www.praymag.com to order.

Revival 101: Understanding How Christ Ignites His People. A primer on revival, written by Dale Schlafer, the head of the National Revival Network, *Revival 101,* gives readers a longing to see a fresh outpouring of God's Spirit on their church. *Revival 101* has exciting stories of revival, and compelling discussion questions to stimulate people's interest in the subject. Go to www.praymag.com for order information.

Purchase Additional Copies of:

READY FOR REVIVAL

A 40-Day Heart Journey Toward the Fullness of Christ

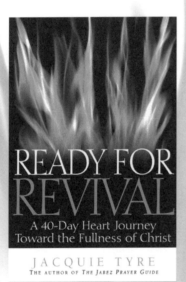

$6*

- *Great guide to pray with your entire church*
- *Better yet . . . pray through this guide with a group of churches*

Order multiple copies and enjoy deep discounts!

QUANTITY	PRICE PER COPY*
2 – 5	$5.40
6 – 24	$4.80
25 -49	$4.50
50 – 99	$4.00
100 +	$3.60

*plus shipping and handling

Pray! Books

ORDER TODAY! Call 1-800-366-7788

(or 719-548-9222) M-F 7am-5pm MST

Offer #6381

If you pray through this guide, you will be changed!
If your church prays through this guide, it will never be the same!

Change the Way You Pray!

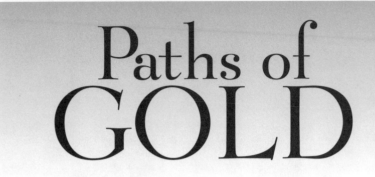

Paths of GOLD

Praying the Way to Christ for Lost Friends and Family

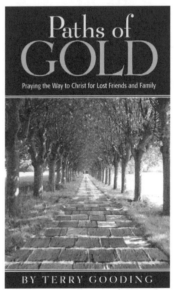

BY TERRY GOODING

$2 single copy
*plus shipping & handling

This powerful, pocket-sized prayer evangelism tool is designed to fuel your prayers for unsaved friends and loved ones! Five themes, 46 Scripture-based kingdom prayers, and space to record how God is moving will keep you praying effectively.

Order multiple copies for your own use or to give away as an encouragement to others. Buy copies for every member of your congregation and watch them get excited about praying for the lost! Deep discounts when you buy more than one!

QUANTITY	PRICE PER COPY*
2 – 5	$1.80
6 – 10	$1.75
11 – 25	$1.50
26 – 99	$1.25
100 – 999	$1.00
1000+	$ .80

ORDER TODAY!
Call 1-800-366-7788
(or 719-548-9222)• 7am-5pm M-F, MST

Offer #6381

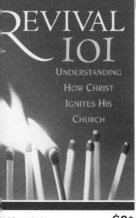

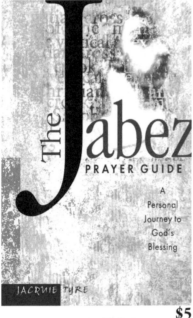

Here's a resource to help you pray with more

Power, Passion, & Purpose

Every issue of *Pray!* will provide outstanding content:

- Powerful teaching by seasoned intercessors and prayer leaders
- Encouragement to help you grow in your prayer life—no matter at what level you are currently
- Exciting news stories on the prayer movement and prayer events around the world
- Profiles on people, organizations, and churches with unique prayer ministries
- Practical ideas to help you become a more effective prayer
- Inspirational columns to stimulate you to more passionate worship of Christ
- Classic writings by powerful intercessors of the past
- And much, much more!

No Christian who wants to connect with God should be without *Pray!*

Six issues of *Pray!* are only $19.97*

(*Plus sales tax where applicable. Canadian and international subscriptions are $25.97.)

Call **1-800-691-PRAY** (or 1-515-242-0297)
and mention code H4PRBKRFR when you place your order.

For information on other prayer tools, Bible studies, and prayer guides
call for a free resource catalog: 719-531-3555